Write It Right

with

Step by Step

by

Edna Mae Burnam

To my grandson, David Bender

ISBN 978-1-4234-3602-7

WILLIS MUSIC

EXCLUSIVELY DISTRIBUTED BY

HAL•LEONARD®
CORPORATION
7777 W. BLUEMOUND RD. P.O. BOX 13819 MILWAUKEE, WI 53213

Visit Hal Leonard Online at
www.Halleonard.com

TO THE TEACHER

The written work in this book is designed to correlate exactly with Edna Mae Burnam's STEP BY STEP—Book Four.

At the beginning of each lesson, at the top of the page, is a notation giving the exact page in the correlated STEP BY STEP book at which the respective WRITE IT RIGHT lessons may be introduced. (Each lesson is planned on the musical steps which have been introduced up to and including this page.)

The WRITE IT RIGHT lessons will both train the student to be accurate and afford the teacher a means of checking the student's comprehension of the musical steps which he or she is learning.

A special effort has been made to incorporate variety in the written work and to choose subject matter which is appealing to the student.

I sincerely hope that the WRITE IT RIGHT lessons will be an enjoyable experience.

Edna Mae Burnam

When the student reaches page 5 of Edna Mae Burnam's STEP BY STEP — Book Four, he is ready to do Lesson One.

3

LESSON ONE

HANGING MOBILE

Decorate the mobile.
Put:

- a **treble clef** in 1
- a **bass clef** in 2
- a **sharp** in 3
- a **flat** in 4
- a **natural** in 5
- a **hold sign** in 6
- a **staccato** in 7
- an **accent** in 8
- an **eighth note** in 9
- an **eighth rest** in 10
- a **quarter note** in 11
- a **quarter rest** in 12

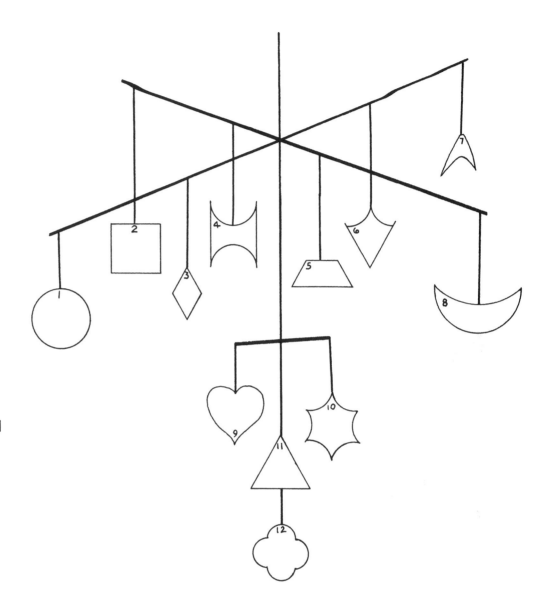

MATCH UPS

Draw a line from the word to the matching example.

tie

phrase

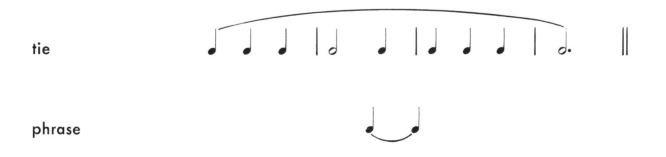

COIN PURSE

This purse has some coins inside.

To find out how many pennies, nickels, dimes, quarters and dollars there are, add the counts of the notes and rests in each line, and put the answer in the box at the end of each line.

	pennies
	nickels
	dimes
	quarters
	dollars

WORD MEANINGS

Write the right meaning for the words in the long boxes.

legato

moderato

QUESTIONS

Does **moderato** mean medium loud?   _____

Is a music sentence called a phrase?   _____

Is a phrase always four measures long?   _____

Does a phrase mark look
    like this?   _____

When the student reaches page 11 of Edna Mae Burnam's STEP BY STEP—Book Four, he is ready to do Lesson Two.

LESSON TWO

THE SKY AND THE SEA

Write the right
letter names in
the boxes for the
notes in the sky
and in the sea.

PHRASES

Here are some
musical sentences.
Put a **phrase mark**
over each sentence.

BAR LINES

Draw bar lines in the right places for this line of notes.

SEA SHELLS

When you hold a sea shell to your ear, you can hear the song of the sea. In each shell below, the sea sings in a different key. Write the right **key signature** in the box by each shell.

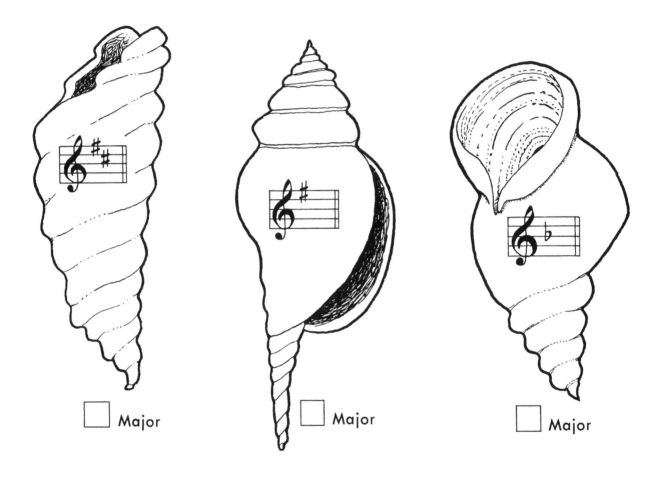

☐ Major   ☐ Major   ☐ Major

QUESTIONS

Does **allegretto** mean to play lively?   _____

Does **moderato** mean to play slow?   _____

Is this a **slur?**   _____

7

When the student reaches page 14 of Edna Mae Burnam's STEP BY STEP—Book Four, he is ready to do Lesson Three.

LESSON THREE

BALLOON

Write the right letter names
of the notes in the boxes.
If you get all of them right, you
may have a ride in the balloon.

ALARM CLOCKS

These alarm clocks are set
to go off in the morning.
Add up the counts of the notes
to find out when the alarms will ring.
Draw in the short hands of the clocks
to indicate the correct time.

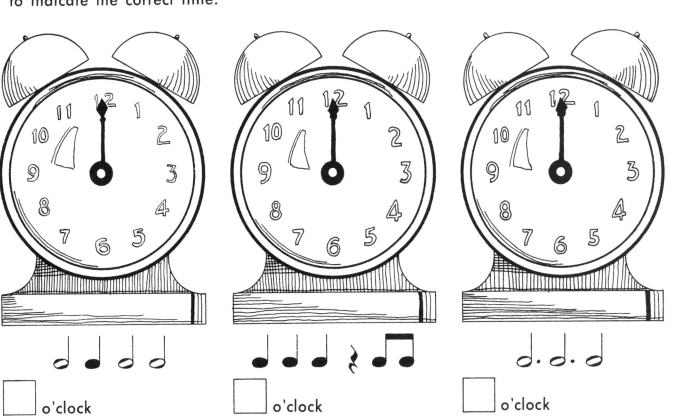

o'clock   o'clock   o'clock

8

WORD MATCH UPS

Draw a line from each Italian word in column one to its English meaning in column two.

One	Two
moderato	smooth
allegretto	gradually slower
andante	gradually louder
crescendo	slowly
ritard	lively
legato	moderately fast
fine	the end

SENTENCES

allegretto

The music is bright and ☐

legato

The cake frosting is very ☐

fine

I will read this book to ☐

QUESTIONS

Is **moderato** faster than **andante**? _____

Is **allegretto** faster than **moderato?** _____

When the student reaches page 21 of Edna Mae Burnam's STEP BY STEP—Book Four, he is ready to do Lesson Four.

9

LESSON FOUR

BIRDS ON TELEPHONE WIRES

Write the letter names of the bird notes in the boxes.

JEWEL BOX

The jewel box contains some jewelry.

Add the counts of the notes and rests to find out how many rings, bracelets, lockets, and earrings there are in the jewel box.

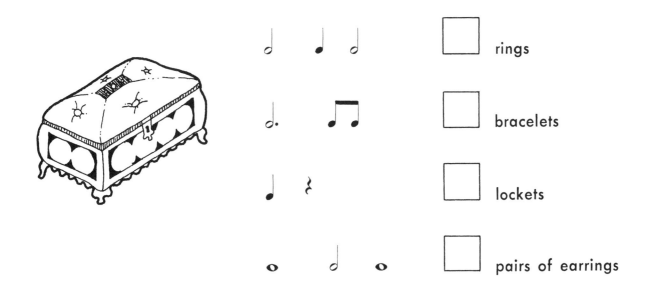

MATCH UPS

Draw a line from each word to the matching example.

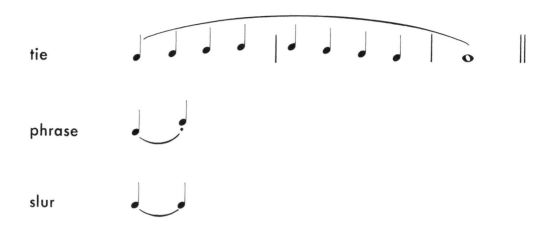

tie

phrase

slur

SENTENCES

Write the right word needed in the boxes.

l.h.

He throws the frisbee with his ⬚.

dolce — — — — — — — — —

The girl is singing ⬚ and ⬚.

andante

The turtle moves ⬚.

allegretto

The radio is playing a ⬚ tune.

QUESTIONS

What is the name of the little short line
that runs through the middle of **MIDDLE C?** _____

What is the name of the note on the second
leger line above the treble staff? _____

What is the name of the note on the first
leger line above the treble staff? _____

When the student reaches page 25 of Edna Mae Burnam's STEP BY STEP—Book Four, he is ready to do Lesson Five.

11

LESSON FIVE
QUILL PEN LETTER

This letter was written with an old fashioned quill pen on parchment-torn paper.
Write the right letter names of the notes in the boxes.
If you get all of them right, you may have a quill pen.

ARCHERY

Draw an arrow from the word or words in the column below to the right place on the target.

moderately fast

slowly

march time

softly and sweetly

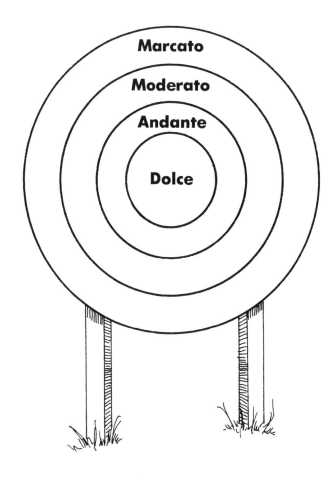

TV

Write the right words needed in the boxes.

allegretto

This TV program is [   ]

This TV program is [   ]

exciting right to the **fine**

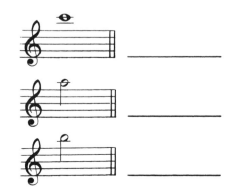

MUSIC BOXES

Each music box is playing a tune in a different key.

Write the right key signature for each one in the boxes.

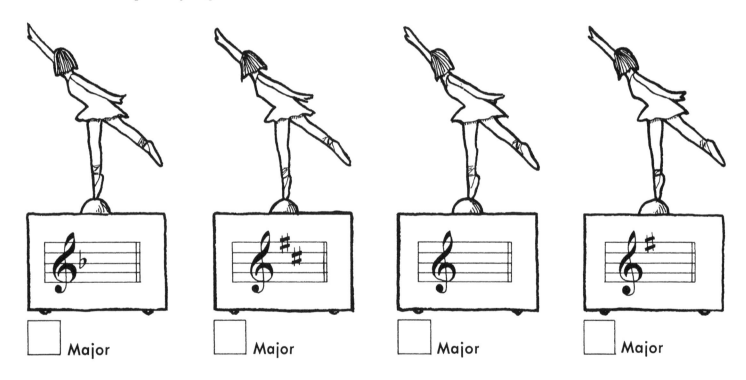

[   ] Major   [   ] Major   [   ] Major   [   ] Major

QUESTIONS

Is this a leger line note? _____

What leger line is this note on? _____

What is the letter name of this note? _____

When the student reaches page 29 of Edna Mae Burnam's STEP BY STEP—Book Four, he is ready to do Lesson Six.

LESSON SIX

FIREWORKS

Write the right letter names of the notes in the boxes.

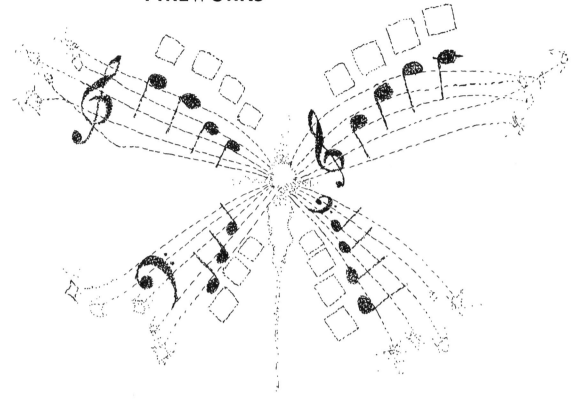

ICE CREAM FREEZERS

By adding up the counts contained in each of these old-fashioned ice cream freezers, you can find out how many quarts they will make.

Write the right answers in the boxes.

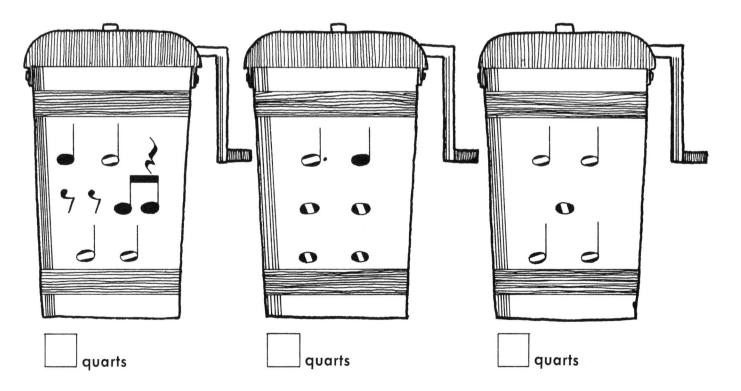

LEAVES

Build a **major triad** on each note.

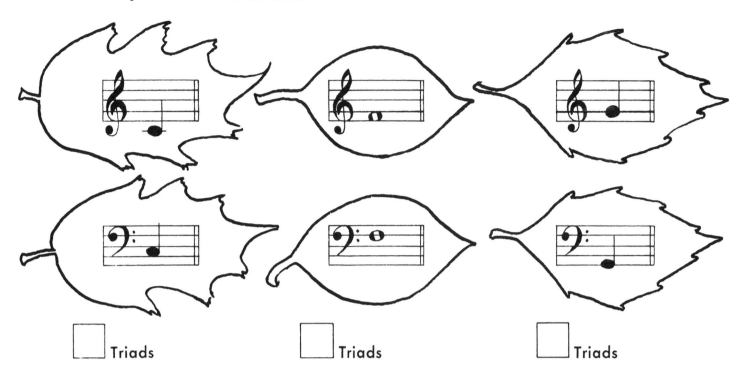

☐ Triads   ☐ Triads   ☐ Triads

KEY SIGNATURE MATCH UPS

Draw a line from each key signature name in column **One** to the match up in column **Two.**

One	Two
D Major	
Bb Major	
F Major	
G Major	

QUESTIONS

What is the name of the key signature that has two flats?   _____ Major

What are the names of the two flats? _____ and _____

What is the name of the key signature that has two sharps?   _____ Major

What are the names of the two sharps? _____ and _____

When the student reaches page 38 of Edna Mae Burnam's STEP BY STEP—Book Four, he is ready to do Lesson Seven.

15

LESSON SEVEN

WITCH'S MAGIC BREW

Write the right letter names of the notes in the boxes.

If you get all of them right, you will have the power to ride through the air on a broomstick — the way witches do!

A SENTENCE

Write in the right names of the notes.
Then, read this sentence aloud.

_ _ S S   N O T _ S   _ R _   _ _ _ P _ S   T H _ S _ _

MATCH UP SIGNS

Draw a line from each word in column **One** to the matching example in column **Two.**

One   **Two**

slur

triplet

tie

phrase

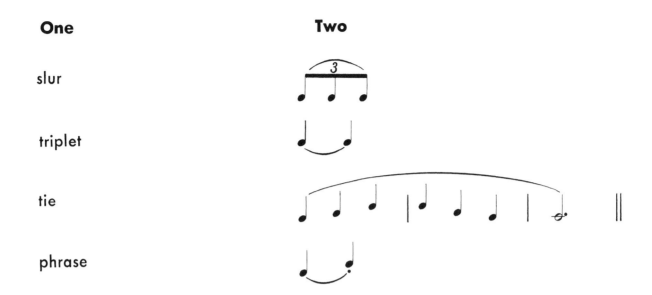

FROG JUMP WINNER

The winner of the Frog Jump made the longest jump of all the frogs.
The notes and rest will tell you how many feet he jumped.
Add up the counts, and write the right answer in the box.

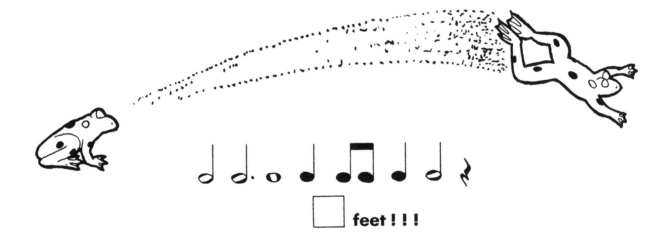

feet ! ! !

QUESTIONS

What is the name of
this leger line note?

How many counts do
these notes receive?

When the student reaches page 46 of Edna Mae Burnam's STEP BY STEP—Book Four, he is ready to do Lesson Eight.

17

LESSON EIGHT

FISHING

Write the right letter names
of the notes.

If you get all of them right,
you catch the fish!

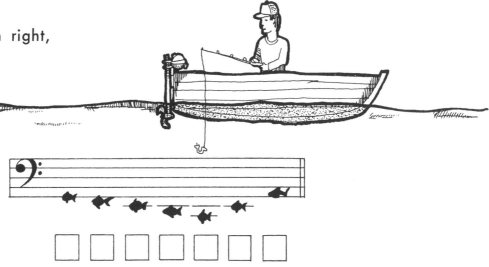

SATELLITE

How many times did this
satellite orbit the Earth?

Add up the counts of the
notes and rests, and put
the right answer in the box.

A HANGING PLANT

Write the right letter names
of the notes in the boxes.
If you get all of them right,
you may have a hanging plant.

TIME SIGNATURE

Write the right time signature for this line of measures.

QUESTIONS

Does **syncopation** mean unusual harmony? _____

Does syncopation mean unusual rhythm? _____

How many counts do these notes receive?  _____

When the student reaches page 48 of Edna Mae Burnam's STEP BY STEP—Book Four, he is ready to do Lesson Nine.

19

LESSON NINE

WATER CARRIER

The notes and rests tell how many
quarts of water there are in the
water jug which this woman is
carrying on her head.
Write the right answer
in the box.

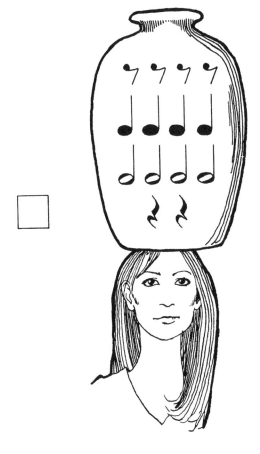

WATERING CAN

Build a **major triad** on the note in each watering can.

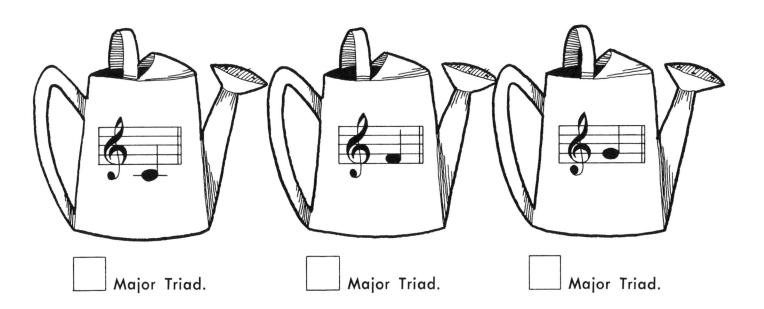

Major Triad.   Major Triad.   Major Triad.

FERRIS WHEEL

Add up the counts of the
notes to find out how
many times the Ferris
Wheel goes around for
one ride.
If you get the answer
right, you may have a ride
on the Ferris Wheel.
Put your answer in
this box.

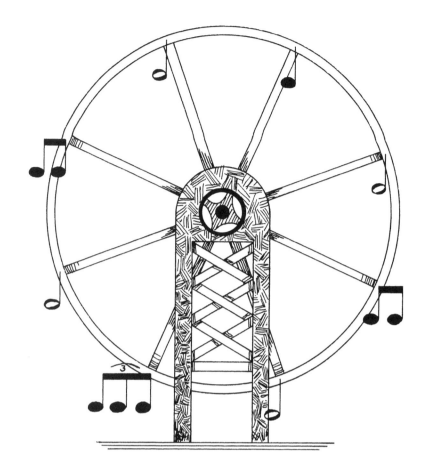

WRITE YOUR NAME

Write your first and last names in music on this staff.

For letters in the music alphabet — draw notes;
for the other letters — write the letter names.

QUESTIONS

Would you play a march **marcato?**   _____

Would you play a lullaby **animato?**   _____

Would you play a piece about firecrackers **dolce?**   _____

Lesson Ten is a review correlated with all of Edna Mae Burnam's STEP BY STEP—Book Four.

LESSON TEN

Write the right letter names of the notes in the boxes.

Draw a line from each box to the right key on the keyboard.

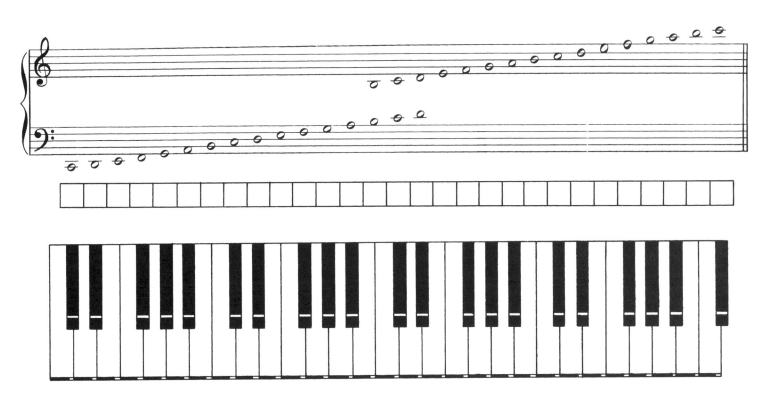

KEY SIGNATURES

Write the right names of the key signatures in the boxes.

☐ Major ☐ Major ☐ Major ☐ Major ☐ Major

The name of the **flat** is ☐

The names of the **flats** are ☐ and ☐

The name of the **sharp** is ☐

The names of the **sharps** are ☐ and ☐

WHIZ QUIZ

Draw a line from each word in column One to the matching example in column Two.

One   **Two**

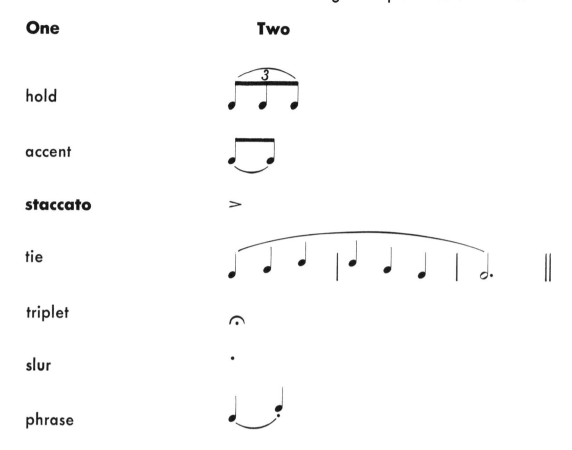

hold

accent

staccato

tie

triplet

slur

phrase

Draw a line from each word in column One to the matching meaning in column Two.

One	Two
andante	the end
dolce	slowly
legato	gradually slower
crescendo	softly and sweetly
moderato	march time
marcato	moderately fast
ritard	gradually louder
fine	smooth

QUESTIONS

Does **syncopation** mean unusual rhythm? _____

May the **key signature** be changed in
  the middle of a piece? _____

Does this sign mean the key of **C major?** _____

Certificate of Merit

This is to certify that

_____

has successfully completed

BOOK FOUR
OF
EDNA MAE BURNAM'S
WRITE IT RIGHT

and is now eligible for promotion to

BOOK FIVE

_____ Teacher

Date _____

Edna Mae Burnam

Edna Mae Burnam (1907–2007) is one of the most respected names in piano pedagogy. She began her study of the instrument at age seven with lessons from her mother, and went on to major in piano at the University of Washington and Chico State Teacher's College in Los Angeles. In 1935, she sold "The Clock That Stopped"—one of her original compositions still in print today—to a publisher for $20. In 1937, Burnam began her long and productive association with Florence, Kentucky-based Willis Music, who signed her to her first royalty contract. In 1950, she sent manuscripts to Willis for an innovative piano series comprised of short and concise warm-up exercises—she drew stick figures indicating where the "real" illustrations should be dropped in. That manuscript, along with the original stick figures, became the best-selling *A Dozen a Day* series, which has sold more than 25 million copies worldwide; the stick-figure drawings are now icons.

Burnam followed up on the success of *A Dozen a Day* with her *Step by Step Piano Course*. This method teaches students the rudiments of music in a logical order and manageable pace, for gradual and steady progress. She also composed hundreds of individual songs and pieces, many based on whimsical subjects or her international travels. These simple, yet effective learning tools for children studying piano have retained all their charm and unique qualities, and remain in print today in the Willis catalog. Visit **www.halleonard.com** to browse all available piano music by Edna Mae Burnam.